The Compile
Barrie C
1925 – .

Published and Book design by
Stephen Cooke

First Published : 24th March 2020
Revision 1.0

ISBN: 9798604061237

In loving Memory

The Compiled Works of Barrie Cooke. 1925 -2011

FOREWARD

This book is something that is very close to my heart. Before my grandparents passed I became very interested in our family tree and history. I found out so much! Generations back we married into the royal line, were owners/founders of the Cyfarthfa Ironwork's at Merthyr Tydfill and responsible for the casting of Big Ben's Bell! Introduced the first steam engine (with Richard Trevithick) and actually found we have a family castle! the list is endless. It was lovely reconnecting and learning so much about my family, after I suffered illness in 2014 which left me permanently disabled and the breakdown of my marriage, I needed something/someone to connect with. My family were and are everything to me. I promised Vicky I would publish these poems and so wish they were here to see the final result.

I want to give a special thanks to Barrie and Vicky's three wonderful children *David, Christoper* and *Grahame* for being an absolutely brilliant source of information and photos, alone with every other family member. bringing many great moments and memories to both Barrie, Vicky and the whole family. Especially for caring and being there when needed for so many of us.

May this book serve as a lasting reminder of the great achievements of Barrie Cooke. Published with the kind permission of his late wife Joan (Vicky) Cooke who sent me the original poems and other literature. After giving me her permission at that time, (but only after her passing) I have included all the poems from there anniversaries and birthdays. Vicky always spoke so highly of Barrie, I really wish I had known them both far more than I did. I have decided to publish these now as I am concerned (with the onset of Stage 3 Cancer and then a diagnose of Unspecified Dementia) that these wonderful memories and poems will just disappear into extinction.

This book contains Barrie's poems written to his wife for there Anniversary's and birthdays. Barrie loved to write, love poems, special events, World War poems and just about anything whenever he felt artistic. A true inspirational and old fashioned gentleman.

All works copyright ©StephenCCooke(2020)

CONTENTS

Chapter 1.   Barrie's Wedding to Joan and their Anniversaries.

        Page 7, Our Wedding Day.
        Page 9, The First (1948)
        Page 10, The Fourth (1951)
        Page 11, The Fifth (1952)
        Page 12, The Sixth (1953)
        Page 12, The Seventh (1954)
        Page 13, The Eighth (1955)
        Page 13, The Ninth (1956)
        Page 14, The Tenth (1957)
        Page 14, The Eleventh (1958)
        Page 15, The Twelfth (1959)
        Page 15, The Thirteenth (1960)
        Page 16, The Fourteenth (1961)
        Page 17, The Fifteenth (1962)
        Page 17, The Seventeenth (1964)
        Page 18, The Eighteenth (1965)
        Page 18, The Nineteenth (1966)
        Page 19, The Twentieth (1967)
        Page 19, The Twenty-first (1968)
        Page 20, The Twenty-second (1969)
        Page 20, The Twenty-third (1970)
        Page 21, The Twenty-fourth (1971)
        Page 22, The Twenty-Fifth (1972)
        Page 23, The Twenty-Sixth (1973)
        Page 23, The Twenty-Seventh (1974)
        Page 24, The Twenty-Eighth (1975)
        Page 24, The Twenty-Ninth (1976)
        Page 25, The Thirtieth (1977)
        Page 26, The Thirty First (1978)
        Page 26, The Thirty Second (1979)
        Page 27, The Thirty Third (1980)
        Page 27, The Thirty Fifth (1982)
        Page 27, The Thirty Sixth (1983)
        Page 28, The Thirty Seventh (1984)
        Page 28, The Thirty Eighth (1985)
        Page 29, The Thirty Ninth (1986)
        Page 30, The Fortieth (1987)
        Page 31, The Forty First (1988)
        Page 32, The Forty Second (1989)

In loving Memory

The Compiled Works of Barrie Cooke. 1925 -2011

          Page 32, The Forty Third (1990)
          Page 33, The Forty Fourth (1991)
          Page 34, The Forty Fifth (1992)
          Page 34, The Forty Sixth (1993)
          Page 34, The Forty Seventh (1994)
          Page 35, The Forty Eighth (1995)
          Page 35, The Forty Ninth (1996)
          Page 36, The Fiftieth (Golden – 1997)
          Page 36, The Fifty First (1998)
          Page 37, The Fifty Second (1999)
          Page 38, The Fifty Third (2000)
          Page 38, The Fifty Fourth (2001)
          Page 39, The Fifty Fifth (2002)
          Page 39, The Fifty Sixth (2003)
          Page 40, The Fifty Seventh (2004)
          Page 41, The Fifty Eighth (2005)
          Page 41, The Fifty Ninth (2006)
          Page 42, The Sixtieth (2007)
          Page 44, The Sixty First (2008)
          Page 44, The Sixty Second (2009)
          Page 44, The Sixty Third (2010)

Chapter 2.   Birthday Poems

          Page 46, Twenty Second
          Page 46, Twenty Forth
          Page 46, Twenty Fifth
          Page 47, Twenty Sixth
          Page 48, Twenty Seventh
          Page 48, Twenty Eighth
          Page 48, Twenty Ninth
          Page 49, Thirtieth
          Page 49, Thirty First
          Page 50, Thirty Second
          Page 50, Thirty Third
          Page 52, Thirty Fourth
          Page 52, Thirty Fifth
          Page 53, Thirty Sixth
          Page 53, Thirty Eighth
          Page 54, Thirty Ninth
          Page 56, Fortieth
          Page 56, Forty First
          Page 57, Forty Second
          Page 58, Forty Third

Page 58, Forty Fourth
Page 58, Forty Fifth
Page 59, Forty Sixth
Page 60, Forty Seventh
Page 60, Forty Eighth
Page 61, Forty Ninth
Page 61, Fiftieth
Page 62, Fifty First
Page 62, Fifty Second
Page 63, Fifty Third
Page 64, Fifty Fourth
Page 64, Fifty fifth
Page 65, Fifty Sixth
Page 66, Fifty Seventh
Page 67, Fifty Eighth
Page 67, Fifty Ninth
Page 68, Sixty Glorious Years
Page 70, Sixty First
Page 70, Sixty Second
Page 71, Sixty Third
Page 72, Sixty Fourth
Page 72, Sixty Fifth
Page 73, Sixty Seventh
Page 73, Sixty Eighth
Page 73, Sixty Ninth
Page 74, Seventieth
Page 75, Seventy First
Page 75, Seventy Second
Page 76, Seventy Third
Page 76, Seventy Fourth
Page 77, Seventy Fifth
Page 77, Seventy Sixth
Page 78, Seventy Seventh
Page 78, Seventy Eighth
Page 79, Seventy Ninth
Page 80, Eightieth
Page 80, Eighty First
Page 81, Eighty Second

APPENDIX and Additional Information

Page 82

In loving Memory

The Compiled Works of Barrie Cooke. 1925 -2011

Chapter 1

Barrie and Joan's Wedding day and anniversaries

OUR WEDDING DAY, JULY 19th 1947

On January 2nd forty four ,
Do you recall that day?
When first I saw you at the door,
"You must be Vicki" was all I could say.

Somehow even then I could see ,
One day you'd be my wife,
Funny is'nt it? you came to tea,
And completely changed my life.

Separations proved our love ,
But we had our share of fun,
I thank Almighty God above ,
For making you the one.

Three and a half years went by,
The happiest of my life,
And on the nineteenth of July,
I made you my wife.

Can I ever forget that wonderful day?
You looked so lovely dear,
To me you'll always be that way,
The memory crisp and clear.

Remember what we did, my love,
We had our photo's done,
Then a taxi to the Cumberland,
Where we had some drinks — not one.

In loving Memory

Lunch at the Castle,
Then time for a blow ,
Tea at Roses,
Then on to a show.
We saw 'Annie Get Your Gun' ,
A really wizard show,
Then off to 13 Albany Street,
A guy's got to sleep you know.

It was our wedding night,
But oh, you little scamp,
Did you have to choose that night,
To get a spot of cramp.

Then off to the Isle of Wight,
To spend our honeymoon,
Everything went off just right,
But it passed away too soon.

Once more we are apart,
But only for a while,
Next month we'll meet again sweetheart,
And I can once more smile.

Our whole life is ahead of us ,
It's up to us to swear,
To make it a life of happiness,
And love beyond compare.

We have so many more happy days in store,
It's fun getting up a home,
Building our heaven chair by chair,
Knowing its our own.

A place only for we two,
Then one day they'll be three,
A little angel just like you,
How happy we will be.

I love you Vicki, only God knows how,
That's one thing that will never change ,
That will always be as now,
And fate will never rearrange.

Now, at last, you are my wife,
Our life's about to start,
The joys, the tears of married life,
Will all be ours sweetheart.

And now my angel, bless you,
And though you may be far away ,
God grant you love me always,
As I love you this day.

THE FIRST (1948)

The golden sands of time speed on,
Just like a fleeting kiss,
Another year has passed us by ,
A year of married bliss.

'Twas the 19th day of the 7th month,
In nineteen forty seven,
That day existed on this earth,
But it seemed to us like heaven.

For on that sweet and lovely day ,
My dearest dreams came true,
Oh, what a glorious thrill it was,
To hear you say do" .

What words can flow from this pen I hold,
Sweet enough to say,
All that lingers in my heart,
Each night and every day.

It's actions now that count, not words,
But I feel so helpless here,
Two thousand miles from you my wife,
And all I hold so dear.

But even though we are apart,
Our love can yet be shown,
By your bearing of a lovely child,
All our very own.

Is my cup of love now full?
Could I love you any more,
I love you more now Vicki dear,
Than I did in days of yore.

Yet how many times did I tell myself,
That selfsame question then,
I know the answer now though dear ,
And it can't be asked again.

The answer is, I know full well,
My cup will never fill,
I've loved you since the day we met,
And know I always will.

So what can I say but 'Thank you" ,
And for the remainder of my life,
I'll try to make a life of joy,
For you, my darling wife.

THE FOURTH (1951)

Do you remember this my love ,
A starry night, a moon above,
A towpath walk, some idle talk,
Do you recall my dear?

A separation, then a meeting,
Golden hours, sweet but fleeting,
A promise and we two were one,
A life of togetherness to come.

Do you remember too my love ,
A thousand miles or more from here ,
Beneath an azure Maltese sky ,
A son was born to you and I.

And now another bless'd event,
A son or daughter heaven sent,
Will bring us joy beyond compare,
A happiness that four can share.

So on this anniversary day,
Four milestones passed along life's way,
What can I say but God grant this,
Be just four of years of bliss.

THE FIFTH (1952)

Five years. Can it be that long?
Passed like the chorus of a song,
Five minutes in the hour of life,
Spent together, man and wife.

Five years and time goes racing on,
Another year had come and gone,
The summer's sun, the winter's snow
In happiness they come and go.

Five years! What happy ones they've been,
Together with every changing scene ,
At home, abroad, anywhere ,
Our love has always lingered there.

Five years, and now we have two sons,
Mischievous, gay, unruly ones,
They harass us from dawn to dawn,
But bless the day that they were born.

And now my darling wife and mother,
(How could I ever love another?)
Bless you for these happy years ,
And sharing of my joy and tears.

And so a toast to you and I ,
May you love me as in days gone by,
Remembering I love you so,
As I did this day five years ago.

THE SIXTH (1953)

A few short lines, a verse or two,
From far away I send to you,
Conveying in my humble way ,
Sincere wishes on this day.

Six years have passed since first we gave,
Our vows to cherish to the grave,
Fate was kind to give to me,
Your love for all eternity.

In those six years came tears and laughter
And through all our married life hereafter ,
Please God we live there you and I,
Modeled on the years gone by.

THE SEVENTH (1954)

It seems to me like yesterday ,
On that nineteenth of July ,
When at my side, I heard you say,
'1 do until 1 die'.

Those five short words have changed my life,
They gave me you, my dear,
From that day you became my wife,
And my destiny was clear.

I love you now as I did then,
I'll always love you so,
For all my life, as on that day,
Just seven years ago.

THE EIGHTH (1955)

Through days of joy and strife,
Of happiness and tears ,
We've been together, man and wife,
Today for eight sweet years.

Eight years. How long ago that seems,
But in a life of bliss,
Of happiness and pleasant dreams ,
As fleeting as a kiss.

So deep in my heart upon this day ,
I wish you joy and laughter,
To live, as fairy tales would say,
Happy ever after.

THE NINETH (1956)

Nine years have passed, how short it seems ,
Yet what has happened in that time?
What memories we have, what dreams ,
To take with us upon life's line.

And along this line, what is in store?
Through all the days and years to come,
May our love remain for evermore ,
May we always be, we two, as one.

Nine years have passed since first we made,
Those vows, our tender love to bide,
They'll last, of that be not afraid,
While we 're together side by side.

And so together let us face,
The future with our children three ,
As in the book of life we trace ,
Another anniversary.

THE TENTH (1957)

Look back, my love, to this same day,
Just ten short years ago,
Through the mist Of , I hear you say,
"My dear, I love you so,"
Young lovers. Oh the world was ours,
The future good and sweet,
We 'd walk a highway strewn with flowers ,
Our happiness complete.

And through the years that dream was mine ,
Your love was all I had,
The days, the months, the years sublime,
Three kids to call me Dad.

Oh, what has happened to us now?
Our skies are overcast,
Can all the happiness we knew,
Be some dream of the past?

I'm still the same, and so are you,
I' 11 always love you so,
Love me darling as you did too,
Just ten short years ago.

THE ELEVENTH (1958)

For eleven years of wedded bliss ,
My thanks to you my love,
For each embrace and loving kiss,
My thanks to you my love.

My thanks sweetheart for all those years,
For David, Grahame, Chris,
My thanks for all the hopes and fears,
We've shared in loving bliss.

For all your loving, tender care,
For every smile and tear,
If only just for being there,
My thanks to you my dear.

THE TWELFTH (1959)

For all the days that make a year,
This day stands apart ,
For on this day, twelve years ago,
Our married life did start.

An anniversary has come again,
Another year has flown,
But our love has always been the same,
I love but you alone.

For passing years will ne'er erase,
A love as great as mine,
Nor time in every passing phase,
Will dim our love sublime.
May happiness and joy be yours,
May love surround your life,
And may I share these golden hours ,
With you, my darling wife.

THE THIRTEENTH (1960)

I remember, years ago,
As clearly as can be ,
Seeing a little dark haired girl,
And saying, "That's for me."

She stood out from the other girls ,
Lovable and sweet,
I gave my heart right there and then,
And laid it at her feet.

We married, and in due course,
As time went flying by,
We raised a little family,
This dark haired girl and I.

Many partings came our way,
Many hours of separation,
But, in their wake, reunion's joys,
Brought ample consolation.

Thirteen years have come and gone,
As fleeting as a dream,
Wonderful, tender, happy years,
Of joy and love serene.

Oh, darling girl, I love you so,
My love will never die,
As through life's winding trail we walk,
My dark haired girl and I.

THE FOURTEENTH (1961)

What can I say that's not been said,
A thousand times before?
What new phrase can I coin instead,
For the girl that I adore.

Words are too conventional ,
We repeat them parrot fashion,
To prove our feeling are intentional,
We write of 'Love' and 'Passion'.

Actions speak the loudest,
But you're much too far away,
To show you I'm the proudest
Of men upon this day.

So instead of touch, accept a word,
Instead of a kiss, a verse,
Remembering the day our hearts were stirred,
By "For better or for worse".

Recall the things we had to say?
The sun shone in the sky,
Remember how we felt that day,
When we married, you and I.

So now we arrive at the fourteenth year,
And again with all my heart,
I wish you joy, my dearest dear,
On this day, from the start.

THE FIFTEENTH (1962)

I miss you more and more it's true
But that's a very good sign,
My loving arms reach out to you,
Across the sands of time.

The joys we shared, right from the start,
The tears and heartaches too,
Will keep us close while we're apart,
Until I'm home with you.

THE SEVENTEENTH (1964)

For love and joy and sweet content,
Three children and a life well spent,
For the memories that this day brings ,
Thank you dear for all these things.

Through summer suns and winter snows.
The grief of loss, the joy of gains,
When every well of hope ran dry ,
Thank you dear for standing by.

Thank you even for the fights,
The kiss when things are put to rights,
You're in my every dream and prayer,
And thank you dear for being there.

Seventeen years ago this day ,
Two youngsters joined hands on the way,
Their way that leads to hope or sorrow,
But dreaming of a bright tomorrow.

Tomorrow's sun shone high above,
And blessed our union and love ,
And for all those years, apart or near,
With all my heart I thank you dear.

THE EIGHTEENTH

How often have I told you,
With heart and words sincere ,
In what regard I hold you,
And how I love you dear.

How often have I thanked you ,
For being what you are,
No one has e 'er outranked you,
You've shone out from afar.

Those times are countless, heaven knows,
But of one thing I am sure,
As each year passes my love grows,
To something good and pure,.

But I can count each year we've spent,
Together you and I,
In happiness and sweet content,
Eighteen have passed us by.

THE NINETEENTH

In all my waking thoughts and dreams,
Laughing, weeping, near or far,
Over mountains, fields and streams,
Vying with the brightest. star.

Ever greater grows my love,
Years have passed and still it spreads,
Upward to the skies above,
Under to the ocean beds.

Darling, on this day I pray,
Endless love will be our lot,
Always lovers, come what may ,
Remembered always — ne'er forgot.

THE TWENTIETH (1967)

God give to man one gift in life,
I know this to be true,
For the day that you became my wife,
His gift to me was you.

Seven thousand three hundred days,
Since first we wed have passed,
Seven thousand three hundred ways,
We've proved our love can last.

It lasted when all around was war,
It's lasted through the peace ,
Through all the trials that lie in store,
Our love will never cease.

Bless you dear heart for that love,
And now we've reached a score,
I pray I'll have, all else above,
Your love for many more.

THE TWENTYFIRST (1968)

For half my life you've been my wife,
Twenty one years to the day,
The 'key of the door' is ours once more ,
In a matrimonial way.

We've come of age, and at this stage,
Our skies are clearing blue,
No more to part again sweetheart,
Our lives begin anew.

Of all those years of joy and tears,
Not one do I regret,
Yet better days in many ways,
Are coming to us yet.

For days, though sweet, are incomplete,
When couples have to part,
But when, at last, those days are passed,
They make another start.

And the change we make will be a break,
From the ways that once we knew,
God grant that we, with this other key,
Find love our whole lives through.

THE TWENTY SECOND (1969)

On this day, I'd like to say,
A heartfelt 'Thank you dear',
To one who shares my joys and cares,
Through past and future years.

I'd like to say, in a humble way,
What your love for me has done,
How being my wife has made my life,
A proud and happy one.

The years have sped since first we wed,
But this, I vow, is true,
A flower cannot change its scent,
Nor I my love for you.

APPRECIATION

THE TWENTY THIRD (1970)

The other day I had a thought,
And said, 'Now, there's a thing',
'How many years since you were caught,
'And gave your wife that ring?'

So calculating in my brain,
I found since first we wed,
(After counting up just once again),
That twenty three had sped.

Now, twenty three and three kids later,
My love is not as such,
No sir. In fact its grown much greater,
And I love you twice as much.

THE TWENTY FOURTH (1971)

Phones are ringing everywhere,
Breakfast trays with roses,
Such excitement in the air,
Disturbing my reposes.

Something brews - I wot not what,
The fuss is all around me,
Involved I am as like as not,
The mystery surrounds me.

My brain begins a – reeling,
We've been through this before,
Not once — I have a feeling,
It's more like twenty four.

Now, with that number, visions flow,
Of wedded blis - a nursery,
My goodness gracious, now I know,
It's our ANNIVERSARY.

And so, once more, it's time to say,
The words I said to you,
On that well beloved, remembered day,
"I love you - 'deed I do."

THE TWENTY FIFTH (1972)
'Silver Wedding Anniversary'

Silver bells in fairy dells,
Silver linings in the sky,
Silver gleams of mountain streams,
Silver days for you and I.

Silver dew drops on the lawn,
Touched by silver rays at dawn,
Silver moonbeams dancing by ,
Silver nights for you and I.

Silver sheen's and silver screens,
Streaks of silver in our hair,
Silver spoons and silver moons,
Silver stands for all that's fair.

And silver are the years that led,
Up to this silver day,
But, golden are the years ahead,
That lead us to our golden day.

THE TWENTY SIXTH (1973)

Did you think you'd never get,
A poem from me dear?
You know I've never failed you yet,
You've had one every year.

And this one's no exception,
Though verily I fear,
'Twill be upon reflection,
A shorter one this year.

But what matters most is not the length,
Of the ode I pen this day,
But the words in the lines and the hidden strength,
Of the feeling they convey.

My love , my dear, grows stronger yet,
On that you can rely,
And, rest assured, I'll ne'er forget,
The nineteenth of July.

THE TWENTY SEVENTH (1974)

I knew that on the day we met,
I'd found a precious pearl,
And there and then I made a bet,
I'd have you for my girl.

And after we'd been going out,
A little while this way,
I decided that, without a doubt,
I'd marry you one day.

So marry you I did and then,
Along came three fine boys,
Who grew up to be three fine men,
And now we miss the noise.

But though they've left, the family grows,
Two wives and now a grandson,
And there' s hope for Chris too, heaven knows,
He really is quite handsome.

From boy and girl, to Mum and Dad,
With the minimum of tears,
And now it's Nan and Granddad,
In twenty seven years.

Yes, all these years have passed away,
Since I wed my favorite girl,
And I wouldn't change a single day,
Nor yet my precious pearl.

THE TWENTY EIGHTH (1975)

Two newly weds with eyes aglow,
Taking in a West End show,
How many years ago was that?
'Twas eight and twenty years ago.

Beneath an azure Maltese sky,
A son was born to you and I,
How many years have gone since then?
Twenty six have passed us by.

Chris was born 'neath leaden skies,
And Grahame took us by surprise,
How many years since then, my love.
Twenty two have gone. Time flies.

Through all these years I've loved you so,
In summer's warmth and winter's snow,
And how long can this love then last?
Until there's no more time to go.

THE TWENTY NINETH (1976)

Well pet, we've gone a good few years,
Along the road of wedded bliss,
We've laughed and chatted, shed some tears,
And stole the occasional kiss.

Sometimes this happy road would fork,
And then we'd have to part,
For a while, in loneliness we'd walk,
Then we'd meet again sweetheart.

Three time we paused along the road,
To collect a little bundle,
Then, bearing a chuckling, smiling load,
Off again we'd trundle.

We've walked a happy, joyous way ,
I and my darling wife,
With many years to walk pray,
To the end of the road of life.

THE THIRTIETH (1977)

On this day, thirty years ago,
Uniformed and proud I stood,
Right by your side; I loved you so,
Prepared to pledge my love for good.

Even though we walked no isle,
And no priest made us man and wife,
Remember how I promised I'll,
Love you while I've breath of life.

Your love for me has made that vow,
Delightfully easy to observe,
And I pray that all the days from now,
Your precious love I still deserve.

TO A PEARL GIRL.

Barrie, Vicki and their sons. Grahame, Christoper and David.

THE THIRTY FIRST (1978)

I often wonder why my fate,
Decided she should be my mate,
She's a pest, a menace and Pete knows what,
But I wouldn't change my lot a jot.

She twists me round her little finger,
The smallest thing she wants, I bring her,
I'm always at her beck and call,
But do I mind? No, not at all.

Sometimes I think in forty four,
When saw her standing at the door,
I should have promptly gone to ground,
But now I'm glad I hung around.

For she's my very breath of life,
A loyal, sweet and loving wife,
And I'm glad that fate decreed that she,
Would want to share her life with me.

THE THIRTY SECOND (1979)

I've picked up my pen full thirty two times,
To write an ode upon these lines,
And place it on your breakfast tray,
On this our very special day.

For every year about this time,
I get my chance with verse and rhyme,
To thank you for the chance you took,
When you changed your name to Mrs Cooke.

And now there's two more Mrs Cooke's ,
Four grandsons with the Cooke' s good looks,
Lovely kids, but you know I sort' a,
Wish that one had been a daughter.

But, never mind, I have a wife,
Who gives me all I want of life,
So I write these lines in appreciation,
To the sweetest girl in all creation.

THE THIRTY THIRD (1980)

This year, the day on which we wed,
Will be spent apart I fear,
Of that, my dear, right up I'm fed,
'Cos I'd rather have you near.

But duty calls, and so sweetheart,
We must go our separate ways,
But it tears my heart that we've to part,
On this our day of days.
But do not despair, you're not alone,
And here I pledge my word,
To wish you on the telephone,
A joyous thirty third.

THE THIRTY FIFTH (1982)

So here we are again my dear,
Once more it is that time of year,
To raise our glasses with a smile,
And reminisce a little while.

Remembering the days gone by,
Since first we stood, young and shy,
And vowed to spend our life together ,
In sunshine or in stormy weather.

We've had the sun, we've had the rain,
But it's one thing I would do again,
For life would be an ebbing tide,
Without my darling by my side.

Thirty five years have come and gone,
And I wouldn't swap a single one,
So if you feel the same way too,
Give us a kiss and say, "I do."

THE THIRTY SIXTH (1983)

One more anniversary day ,
Another signpost in life's span,
We've passed a few upon the way,
Since our married life began.

Each one special as the last,
Another link formed in the chain,
Another year is in the past,
Another born again.

Remember when you changed your name?
Remember how it all began?
Remember how the boy and girl became ,
The woman and the man?

So on this happiest of days,
To celebrate the day we wed,
We think of the past and the part it plays,
In all the years ahead.

THE THIRTY SEVENTH (1984)

Thirty seven years. Oh my,
Time has flown and passed us by,
But the fleeting years have touched us so,
And caused our love to bloom and grow.

In spring the buds have only just begun,
To reveal the promise of the fruit to come,
It needs rain and sun and lots of luck,
Before the fruit is ripe to pluck.

Our love has weathered every storm,
Is strong and in mature form,
And may it always be the way,
It is on this our special day.

THE THIRTY EIGHTH (1985)

Thirty eight, gee ain't that great,
Years both good and naughty,
I can't believe that at this rate,
It'll very soon be forty.

But, taken by and large, I think,
Time has dealt us fairly,
We've taken up life's cup to drink,
And faced the future squarely.

We've never rolled in the jolly old gold,
But we've never gone without,
Our union has been blessed thrice-fold,
And our love was ne'er in doubt.

Memories of all those years,
Together we can share,
And during all those hopes and fears,
Thank you dear for being there.

THE THIRTY NINTH (1986)

Thirty nine, sweetheart mine,
Now please don't think me naughty,
But in another year, I fear,
The number will be forty.

Now, thirty nine is very fine,
with still a youthful sound,
But forty is the fateful line,
We cannot skirt around.

Now, if the sage should speak of age ,
And count the years in birthdays,
The fortieth would be a gauge,
Measured in spreading girth days.

But here, my dear, we speak I fear,
Of anniversaries instead,
The wedded thirty ninth is here,
The dreaded fortieth lies ahead.

So on this day, let's kneel and pray,
That the years ahead may prove,
An endless play upon this day,
Like a needle stuck in a groove.

But standing still or flying past,
Be the years be many or few,
I'll cherish each one to the last,
If I can spend them all with you.

THE FORTIETH (1987)

Nineteen forty seven. How will history record it?
The things you couldn't buy, even if you could afford it,
Will they mark the coldest winter going on without a break?
Or the longest, hottest summer which followed in its wake.

The hoardings hiding bomb sites, the rubble and the pits ,
The legacy of war and the horrors of the blitz,
Food was scarce and so was coal , nationalization here to stay ,
The world dismissed us saying, 'The Brits have lost their way.

Business slumped, 'Export,' they cried, 'export or we die. '
Historians will ponder and shake their heads and sigh,
And wonder how a nation that had faced its finest hour,
Staunch and brave and smiling, could watch it all turn sour.

We'd won the war and lost the peace, the Empire was a—
crumbling,
Those hopes and lofty visions had all come down a—tumbling ,
An Iron Curtain had descended to cut off east from west,
They spoke of nuclear war, radiation and the rest.

The transistor then was new, the Biro pen was spawned,
The Tories in the wilderness, the Socialist day had dawned,
Theatreland was full of Yanks, their shows were everywhere,
'Annie Get Your Gun' and 'Oklahoma' too was there.

But history will not record the nineteenth of July,
When we stood before the Registrar, young and very shy,
He spoke to us in solemn tones; we answered, 'Yes, I will',
We kissed and, for a moment, the world and time stood still.

No, they'll not record that day that our marriage had begun,
They'll not record the happiness, the gaiety, the fun,
The drinks, the food, the show, the humble bridal suite,
They'll not record, thank God, those hours in Albany Street.

But, always I'll remember and time cannot erase,
The bitter, sweet memories of those far distant days,
Those days are now gone, forty years have slipped by,
But still I shall love you 'till the day that I die'.

THE FORTY FIRST (1988) - REMEMBERING

In life's busy round, what joy can be found,
To pause and remember a while,
The things that we've done, the joy and the fun,
The moments that passed with a smile.

The things that we've seen, the places we've been,
The adventures we've had on the way,
The plans that we've laid, the friends we have made,
Are with me in memory today.

I remember the greetings, those wonderful meetings ,
On steam-filled railway stations ,
The clanking, the clatter, the laughter, the chatter,
The joy on those short vacations.
I remember the toys that we bought for the boys,
Sledge rides in the snow,
The thrills and the spills, as we sped down the hills,
Our faces all aglow.

I remember the fun that we had in the sun,
Basking beneath skies of blue,
I remember the joy, when I held my first boy,
I remember the joy, how much I love you.

So much to remember, in life's chill November,
Since the day you became my dear wife,
But with you by my side, my love will abide,
And endure for the rest of my life.

THE FORTY SECOND (1989)

There was a little girl,
I met one lovely day,
Many long years ago,
I took a fancy to her,
And decided I would woo her,
And determined I would be her steady beau.

so when I knew her better,
I wrote a little letter,
And then in rhyme and verse ,
I asked her to improve my life,
And be my ever loving wife,
For better or for worse.

Time has flown,
The boys have grown,
But this for sure I know,
I love her now,
As I loved her then,
Many long years ago.

THE FORTY THIRD (1990)

Please forgive the brevity,
And, perhaps, a touch of levity,
But of time I haven't got a lot,
Because this date I near forgot.

With dust a few more days to go,
With work piled up and pressing so,
I 'm squeezing this twixt twelve and one,
After my half hour's lunch is done.

So, happy anniversary dear,
May we two be always near,
And love eternal fill our cup,
Err, sorry pet, my time is up.

FORTY FOURTH (1991)

What have I done to deserve you?
So faithful, so kind and so true,
What can I do to serve you?
For all the good things that you do.

How can I ever repay you?
For the care and attention you give,
What can I say but - hey you!
You're the reason that I want to live.

For all the years that I known you,
You've been steadfast and faithful to me,
because of this, I've been true too,
And never once yearned to be free.

So on this day above any other,
Memories flood into my brain,
Of a lover, a wife and a mother,
And the years I would live once again.

And on this day we re-pledge our love dear,
And have a happy day too.
Remembering that above all else dear,
To ourselves we shall always be true.

In loving Memory

THE FORTY FIFTH (1992)

From nineteen forty seven to nineteen ninety two,
The years have come and gone ,
And the colour, dear, this year is blue,
Of our anniversary stone.

The sapphire flashing flames of ice,
Stands for all that's cold,
Forty five years have come and gone,
And now we're getting old.
But my love for you is warm as it was ,
All those years ago,
And this you know, my dear, is because,
I've always loved you so.

THE FORTY SIXTH (1993)

What can I say that's not been said before?
I love you as I did in days of yore,
Age and time cannot erase ,
The ardour of that youthful craze.

So now upon this special day ,
I pen these words once more to say,
Even if I had it in my power,
I wouldn't change a singe hour.

THE FORTY SEVENTH (1994)

We met in war and married in peace,
In nineteen forty seven,
The family's grown, the joys we've known,
Are our little bit of heaven.

Half the century has elapsed,
Since we said 'I do',
The days we've spent in sweet content,
Bear memories for we two.

So raise your glass and drink a toast,
To the days that lie before,
May they pass serene and ever green,
As they did in days of yore.

THE FORTY EIGHTH (1995)

Thumbing through the book of time ,
Reading every. precious line,
Understanding what they mean,
Every nuance and every theme.

Living all those golden hours ,
Of the happy marriage that is ours,
Virtually a lifetime spent,
Every day in sweet content.

For all these things I love you dear,
For being true and ever near,
And for giving me the chance to say,
Thank you on this special day.

THE FORTY NINTH (1996)

By time's endless ribbon we've come,
Full circle to the day we were wed,
Back to our island in the sun,
Back to the nuptial bed.

Back to the time when a boy and a girl,
Honeymooned on this spot,
Those days we spent in a joyous whirl,
Will never be forgot.

So many years have passed since then,
My memory holds scenes fresh and green,
Of the rich, full life we've had since when,
We last viewed, this honeymoon Scene.

And so, among the ghosts of the past,
Together with things we revere,
We remember those days and a love that would last,
And a toast to our forty ninth year

THE FIFTIETH (GOLDEN – 1997)

Looking back on the miles of track that go to make a marriage,
We've traveled long, we've traveled far in our matrimonial carriage,
For Marriage is like a journey taken by a train,
Its passage is remorseless as it ploughs through sun and rain,
Sometime it stops at stations and lingers for a space,
Familiar faces fade away and new ones take their place,
Then, smoothly as a flowing stream, it slowly leaves the station,
Gathers speed and thunders on to its final destination.

Our journey begins on a July day in nineteen forty seven,
With the words, 'I do,' we board the train - destination heaven.
Full fifty years we've traveled now upon this marriage ride,
And I thank the Lord who brought us here, together, side by side.

Now, as our Golden Station drops away, I ask no more than this,
We continue on our journey in matrimonial bliss,
And, maybe if the Lord is kind, and all things being fine,
We'll reach that Diamond Station, the next upon the line.

To my Golden Girl, with my love and gratitude for sharing your life with me.

The sands of time drain slowly through,
The hourglass of life,
Each golden grain a memory of you my darling wife,
And included in that growing pile,
A love that makes it all worthwhile.

THE FIFTY FIRST (1998)

I can't believe that all those years,
Have passed since first we wed,
The things we've done, our hopes and fears,
How quickly time has sped.

Kaleidoscopic pictures go coursing through my brain,
A montage of our happy life together,
Oh, to freeze those moments and live them once again,
Those precious time through calm and stormy weather.

And if I could choose a special day,
To relive in my life,
I'd choose that day I heard you say,
You'd be my darling wife.

And now today we can safely say,
Our vows we made with hearts a-glow,
Still hold true as they did that day,
Just fifty one short years ago.

THE FIFTY SECOND (1999)

Life is a lottery, or so it seems ,
Especially when choosing the girl of one's dreams,
From the moment a boy is aware of the lasses,
He begins to preen and make amorous passes,
Then, as girls come and go, and he still seeks life's goal,
He'll yearn for the one that will capture his soul.

Then, perhaps, with a little luck he'll meet,
The girl who will sweep him off his feet.
But how will he know that this girl he's just met,
Is the one he can never, ever forget?
Most times he wont but, once in a while ,
Perhaps it's her nature, maybe her smile.

He'll know for certain he'll make her his wife,
And so she'll remain for the rest of his life.
This happened to me in the year forty four,
As soon as I saw her at the door,
Fifty five years have passed since that day,
And we've been together, come what may,
But, I know now for sure, deep down in my heart,
On that fateful day, chance too played its part.

THE FIFTY THIRD (2000)

Thank you for coming once to tea,
Thank you for wanting to marry me ,
Thank you for the many joys,
Thank you for three lovely boys.

Thank you for the hours of pleasure,
Memories I'll always treasure ,
And in circumstances foul and fair,
Thank you just for being there.

Thank you for being a steadfast wife,
Your company on the path of life,
And when I 'm down and feeling blue,
Thank you just for being you.

THE FIFTY FOURTH (2001)

Once more I take up pen to write,
An ode in celebration of the time,
We'd be together, come what might,
And I was yours and you were mine.

Those days now seem like a dream,
And we've kept our vows through night and day,
So many memories now they seem,
To blur with time and fade away.

Fifty four years we've been together,
Wonderful, happy years I 'd say,
So my wish is now and will be forever,
Have a happy celebration day.

THE FIFTY FIFTH (2002)

Well I'm blessed, I do not jest,
We're going to have a blessing,
Over the years of hopes and fears,
We've kept each other guessing,
Whether or not we two old dears,
will have a simple blessing,
But now the time has come at last,
We've done the deed, the Father's been,
What's more to be done, remains to be seen.

Over the years we've built,
A disturbing sense of guilt,
Over our civic wedding,
But now we can set the record straight,
Now before it gets too late,
And we know where we are heading.

The hall is booked, buffet and punch,
Drinks laid on for the lucky bunch,
The family's coming, friends are too,
A good old get together, we have so very few.

So, a happy fifty fifth my dear,
With relatives and friends so near,
Pucker up and don't be blue,
We've made a lifetime's dream come true.

THE FIFTY SIXTH (2003)

We're going on our holidays,
Let's hope we have some jolly days,
But it all depends you'll find,
On whether the weather is bad or kind.

But at least there's one good day in store,
Our Anniversary, who could ask for more,
We'll toast our fifty sixth this year,
Good wine, good food and you my dear.

Fifty six is a long, long time,
Since the day you said that you'd be mine,
God grant we'll be together still,
When the time has come to pay the bill.

THE FIFTY SEVENTH (2004)

Fifty seven years today, my how the time has passed away,
In 1926 to be precise a little girl was born — how nice,
To think that 21 years ahead you'd be my wife,
The one I'd adore for the rest of my life.

Times have come and times have went,
The years together we have spent,
Have seen such joy and sweet content,
Three boys we've had, no more,
The first was born on Malta's shore,
The second in a hospital bed,
The third at home and I think I said,
"Why couldn't it have been a girl instead" ,
But with his cheeky smile and dear ways,
He gave us many happy days.

Our relationship has cemented by the passage of time,
Happy anniversary sweetheart mine.

THE FIFTY EIGHTH (2005)

There is a story to be told,
It unfolded in days of old,
When fate brought two young folks together ,
They married and helped tie the tether,
One that was unbroken throughout their lives,
Their love and happiness still survives ,
Throughout their long and happy lives,
Fifty eight years have passed us by,
My goodness, how time does fly ,
A montage of images flash before my eyes,
Out honeymoon, the Maltese isles,
Where our first dear son was born,
At two a.m. in the early morn,
Celle, Gutersloh, happy days,
We lived our lives as in a haze,
Binbrook and Beaumont Drive ,
It was good to be alive,
Now our anniversary day is here,
I wish you happiness and love sincere,
Bless you darling for sharing your life with me,
May the rest of our days be as happy and free,
Now that two hearts are still blended,
My story, thank God, is not yet ended.

THE FIFTY NINTH (2006)

From bygone days ,
Two young folks gaze ,
Out of a photograph frame
Unchanging throughout the days ,
They both look just the same.

It was their wedding day you see,
Embarking on an unknown sea,
Not knowing what lies ahead,
Not the slightest fear or dread,
But life was good to both of us,
We muddled through without much fuss.

I love you now as I did then,
A long time ago, though I remember when,
I stroked your face with a tender touch,
That tells you I loved you very much,
Now the time draws near for me to depart,
Happy anniversary to you sweetheart .

May God keep you in his tender care,
And whenever you want me I'll be there,
Loving you as I've always done,
God bless you darling, dearest one.

THE SIXTIETH (2007)

Well, the day is here at last,
Looking down through all those years,
To a day so long in the past,
It's shrouded in the midst of joy and tears,
It was a day in nineteen forty four,
You stood like a vision at the door,
That day we met will always live.

In my memory through all the days that God may give,
You said,'I've come to tea' ,
I thought, 'Aye aye, that's for me',
We hit it off right from the start,
And soon you were my true sweetheart,
We wed in nineteen forty seven.

Our first step on the ladder to heaven,
As soon as we had left the alter,
I dragged you off to live in Malta,
There was born the first of our three boys,
Sturdy lads who gave us many joys,
Our silver wedding day was spent,
With Edith and Alex in sweet content,
Our golden wedding came along,
Fifty years, still going strong.

A day spent with family and friends,
But this is not where the story ends,
Another signpost is on the way,
It's our diamond wedding day ,
So here we are again in celebratory mood,
With music and dancing and lots of food.

Sixty years we've lived together,
Through happy days and stormy weather,
But I wouldn't change a single one,
Not now nor through all the days to come,
Let's hope there are many more,
And so my love, have a happy day,
One that you can treasure upon life's way,
May it stand out from the rest,
As good as, If not the best.

In loving Memory

THE SIXTY FIRST (2008)

Time has sped by fast,
It's our sixty first at last,
Sixty one years since we were wed,
We're older now and time has sped,
Three boys, now grown up with wives,
Apart from us, living their own lives,
So let's take life while we may,
And have a happy anniversary day.

THE SIXTY SECOND (2009)

There comes a time when my thoughts run dry,
Am I getting old?? Oh, no says I,
My little grey cells are working alright,
It's just that I can't find anything to write,
Thousands of words have been written,
Since that day when first I was smitten,
The dictionary only holds so much,
So all I can say to my dear old dutch,
In words so simple, plain and sincere,
Is a happy sixty second year.

THE SIXTY THIRD (2010)

64 Years were spent together,
Through sunny days and stormy weather,
For all these years, you've been the best of wives,
And may it continue so for the rest of our lives.

Barrie's last anniversary poem before his death.

Never losing faith,
Forever loving,
never looking back,
A loving Father and Husband.

A true inspiration to all his family and friends.

17th December 1925 – 11th September 2011
Barrie Cooke.

Chapter 2

Birthday Wishes

In loving Memory

TWENTY SECOND

Birthday greeting, fond and true,
My darling wife I send to you,
With happiness and love sincere,
That's my wish for you my dear.

And though we may be far apart,
You'll always be within my heart,
And through your twenty second year,
You'll always find me ever near.

Cherishing your love for me,
As I have ever done
Praying that each year may be ,
A lovable and happy one.

TWENTY FORTH
(FROM CYPRUS TO MALTA)

Through endless tracts of sea and blue,
Over desert wastes and hill,
This birthday message comes to you,
From one who loves you still.

May golden hours follow you,
And happiness sublime ,
May love attend you, sweet and true,
Until the end of time.

TWENTY FIFTH

The road of life winds on and on,
Another year has come and gone,
Another milestone on the way,
Marks this, your twenty fifth birthday.

The dearest dreams you visualise,
I'll do my best to realise,
The proving of my love for you,
Will be my aim my whole life through.

So take my hand as off we go,
Along life's road of joys and woe,
My wish for you will be this year,
Good luck, God speed and bless you dear.

TWENTY SIXTH

A generation come and gone,
A season in life's year,
The spring we knew has now passed on,
And summertime is here.

May summer with its skies of blue,
Its tranquil nights and carefree days,
Unfold for you a life anew,
And happiness be yours always.

In loving Memory

TWENTY SEVENTH

Some words to you in verse impart,
Greetings on this day ,
A birthday message from the heart,
In my own peculiar way.

It tells you that I love you so,
As I have always done,
Though years may come and years may go,
My love will linger on.

On this your twenty seventh year,
May you realise the dreams you cherish,
God grant you never shed a tear,
And our love will never perish.

TWENTY EIGHTH

Once again I'm not too late,
Do you think that I'd forget this date?
To wish you now you twenty eight,
A happy birthday dear.

May the coming year bring joy to you,
The path of life run straight and true,
May your troubles all be small and few,
In your eight and twentieth year.

And so my wish to you is this,
A perfect year of joy and bliss,
From Daddy, David, Grahame, Chris,
A happy birthday dear.

TWENTY NINTH

May golden days be yours my dear,
Throughout this coming year ,
May every passing hour,
Bring joy and much good cheer.

Your birthday falls in early spring,
When Nature wakes anew ,
May this occasion be symbolic,
And springtime follow you.

May the sun peep through your window pane ,
Each morning you awake,
May skies of blue smile down on you,
Without a single break.

God bless you dear, you 're twenty nine,
Come, take my hand and then,
Let's walk together, side by side,
And ne'er look back again.

THIRTIETH

If I should tell in prose so fair,
The fullness of my heart,
No single word could I find there,
My message to impart.

'Tis a simple one, yet so profound,
That words cannot assay,
The happiness I wish you,
Upon this blessed day.

No poet I, and yet I'll try,
In prose and verse to say,
May all your future birthdays vie,
For the sweetness of this day

THIRTY FIRST

A birthday card I bring to you,
It's not, I know, the thing to do,
I know you like to read apart,
A birthday message from my heart.

But messages, however tender,
Always seem to lose their splendor,
And seems so very insincere,
When penned by other hands I fear.

So may I now, in my own sweet way,
Convey my prayer for you this day,
Good luck, good health and lots of fun,
On this the day you're thirty one.

May each successive year unfold,
Happiness and joy untold,
And may my birthday wish to you,
Remain throughout your whole life through.

THIRTY SECOND

Once more a birthday verse I pen,
As I have done each year ,
To wish you now, as I did then,
A happy birthday dear.

As each year passes, one by one,
With their store of joy and tears,
May happiness and lots of fun,
Be yours throughout the years.

May gentle breezes stroke your hair,
May sunshine light your days,
And in the dark of night may there,
Be one With you always.

One who loves you as I do,
Who tries with all his might,
To give you joy your whole life through,
A lifetime of delight.

So once again this wish I bring,
Time honored and sincere,
Have, above all anything,
A happy birthday dear.

THIRTY THIRD

Last night a birdie said to me,
'Tomorrow, Vicki's thirty three,'
I cocked an eye and said, so what!
A lot of presents she has got'

He gave me a reproachful stare,
And said, 'Look at you sitting there,
Watching telly, drinking beer,
Never thinking of your wife dear.

'Set pen to paper - never shirk,
This little duty - get to work,
Exercise that sleepy brain,
And compose a birthday ode again.

I stared at yonder bird aghast,
But, cowed beneath this withering blast,
I switched the telly off and then,
I reached for paper and a pen.

For many moments sat I there,
But I could only sit and stare,
No ideas came, no notions bright,
I really was most dim tonight.

But then, in a blinding flash of light,
I knew just what I had to write,
I knew that in my own sweet way,
There was but one thing I could say.

In loving Memory

So, stripped of all the frills and verse,
Short and maybe rather terse,
But from my heart, dear, none the less,
'A happy birthday, sweet, God bless.

THIRTY FOURTH

Once more the time has come to say ,
A happy birthday dear ,
A wish to guide you on your way,
Through yet another year.

May every hour of every month,
Bring happiness and joy,
May it be a year of triumph,
That nothing may destroy.

This birthday is your thirty fourth,
A youngster yet forsooth!
Many a year will sally forth,
Before you lose your youth.

So, may laughter be your constant friend,
May love be ever near,
And may I help you to this end,
For now and ever dear.

THIRTY FIFTH

Although we're in a foreign land,
Many miles apart,
I bring again, with pen in hand,
Birthday greetings my sweetheart.

Once again it's birthday time,
And ever as before,
I give a verse in prose or rhyme,
To the girl that I adore.

But, goodness! what a way to spend,
This bright and happy day,
I wish that were there to lend,
A hand to make you gay.

So darling please accept instead,
This thought and wish sincere,
That though this day be spent in bed,
'Twill be a nice one dear.

THIRTY SIXTH

Awake my love your birthday morn,
Is once more on the scene,
On this the day that you were born,
Your wishes reign supreme.

Your dear old dad and all the band,
Are here to do your bidding,
Today your wish is our command,
Perhaps you think I'm kidding?

Shall we polish, wash the dishes,
Clean the windows, scrub the floors?
Just tell us dear what your wish is,
Detail off the household chores.

Because today is yours, my pet,
The boys and hubby too,
Will make this one the best one yet,
Especially for you.

And that the wish 'A happy day',
May mean much more to you,
We'll try, my love, in our little way,
To make it all come true.

THIRTY EIGHTH

When Mother Nature wakes anew,
And winter season's past,
And larks sing soaring in the blue,
And warmth returns at last.

When soft spring breezes melt the snow,
And sparkling waters leap ,
And hibernates their faces show,
Awake at last from winter's sleep.

'Tis then my love when flowers abound,
Their petals to unfurl,
That spring's sun rose one day and found,
A springtime baby girl.

And so to celebrate this day,
Each year about this time,
I write the words I wish to say,
To you in verse and rhyme.

To wish you all your heart's desire,
Call, and I'll be nigh,
To see that nothing you require,
Will ever pass you by.

And now, a happy birthday dear,
And many more to come,
God grant I'll be for ever near,
To you, my dearest one.

THIRTY NINTH (BIRDSONG)

This morning, gazing at the sky,
That endless vault of blue above,
My thoughts wing and home did fly,
To be beside the one I love.

And then from yonder tree there sprang,
A joyful sound - a happy note,
Perched up high, a sparrow sang,
Music pouring from his throat.

And then a meadow lark on high,
Joined the chorus, skyward winging,
Pigeons warbling nearby,
Set the thrushes sweetly singing.

And as they sang, each in their way,
Of happiness and joy complete ,
I thought, 'How wonderful if they,
Could take a message to my sweet.

And so I asked a passing dove,
To gather all his feathered kind,
'Please fly,' said I, 'to the one I love,
And convey the words I have in mind.

And then from every tree around,
They rose to populate the sky,
Drenched in sweet, cascading sound,
I watched them, ever southward fly.

Over river, stream and burn,
Over city, field and hill,
Fly on! straight on, and never turn,
'Til you reach her windowsill.

So, on your birthday morning dear,
Like me, gaze upward at the skies,
Listen well and you will hear,
The music swell and rise.

And read then in that symphony,
My message, loud and clear,
The wishes that they bring from me,
'A happy birthday dear.'

In loving Memory

FORTIETH

When gentle spring bursts on the land,
And loosens winter's icy hand,
When all the world begins anew,
This season dear belongs to you.

When dormant creatures from their nest,
Rise sleepy eyed from winter's rest,
When blossoms bloom and seed is sown,
This season is your very own.

Yours, because one day in spring,
Nature did a wonderous thing,
From her endless round of toil and whirl,
She paused to make a baby girl.

And so, each year, at springtime's gate,
We celebrate a birthday date,
May lifetime's skies be blue and clear,
And springtime be for ever near.

FORTY FIRST

What can I wish you on this day,
That has not been wished before?
What special thought, what can I say?
For words at best are poor.

And a wish is but a heartfelt thought,
As nebulous as dreams,
Ever chasing, never caught,
Like bursting bubbles; scattered schemes.

So when at times you're feeling low,
And things are getting rough,
And life deals yet another blow,
A wish is not enough.

And so, my love, today I bring,
No wishes, but a vow,
To give to you most everything,
I wish for you right now.

And top of all the list they'll be,
A tender love and true,
And from this love will spring, you'll see,
All that I wish for you.

FORTY SECOND

Oh, woe is me, 'tis birthday time,
Once more my pen I raise,
To greet this day in verse and rhyme,
With songs of joy and praise.

The words are there, the rhyme quite clear,
I gaily start to write,
But wait. By gum! what's this I hear?
My face has gone quite white.

'Tis Mother's day as well they say,
So, along with birthday wishes,
The family's clobbered, come what may,
With the housework and the dishes.

So spare a thought for one and all,
As they labor, please remember,
Dad's wishing Father's day would fall,
On the seventeenth of December.

FORTY THIRD

Of all the days that go to make,
The fullness of a year,
This is the one, make no mistake,
Of most importance dear.

For without this day there' d be no you,
And life would be quite tricky,
For where'd we be, what would we do?
Without our little Vicki.

Just three lost sheep, that's what we'd be,
With no one there to guide us ,
In fact, I think there'd just be me,
Without you here beside us.

And so you see why on this day,
My thoughts are put to rhyme,
To wish you joy along the way,
For this and every birthday time.

FORTY FOURTH

Once again it's birthday time,
And here's a note to say that I'm,
All agog and eager to,
Wish you joy the whole year through.

May all your hopes and dreams mature ,
May every problem have a cure,
And if things don't turn out as planned,
I'll be right there to lend a hand.

And now a birthday kiss for you,
A happy day and presents too,
With lots of lovely things in store,
Throughout the year you're forty four.

FORTY FIFTH

The days and months have flown away,
Flowers and sun proclaim,
Winter's past, it's spring at last,
And birthday time again.

Presents piled upon the bed,
Her breakfast on a tray,
Come sleepy head, the time has fled,
It's the twenty fourth today.

Eat your breakfast quickly,
Or late today I'll be,
For I must behold, as the gifts unfold,
Your face alight with glee.

I love you happy birthday girl,
And wish you joy galore,
'Til I take my pen to write again,
A birthday rhyme once more.

FORTHY SIXTH

With the Stratford bard I can't compete,
And wifely birthdays aren't complete,
Without an ode(ious) rhyme to greet,
Her on her birthday morn.

So, furrowed brow and pen in hand,
No easy rhymes pour forth as planned,
In verse production I'm out -Nanned,
She writes copiously!

But inspiration casts its seed,
Slowly first, then gathering speed,
The verses form for her to read,
On her birthday morn.

These verses written from the heart,
Set these poems far apart,
From the normal birthday greeting art,
They're written with sincerity.

And this has just one end in view,
To pass a wish from me to you,
Ever fresh and ever new,
'A happy birthday dear. '

In loving Memory

FORTY SEVENTH

Today's a most important date,
'Tis Vicki's birthday see,
It's one we always celebrate,
With a rhyme or verse from me.

No card from me will e 'er adorn,
Her shelf, which from a shop was bought,
These artifacts she'd treat with scorn,
And berate me for a heartless wart.

So, ever year about this time,
With furrowed brow and vacant look,
You'll find me working on a rhyme,
To go in Vicki's birthday book.

And all these rhymes, in many ways,
Have expressed a wish sincere,
That peaceful nights and happy days,
Will be yours throughout the year.

FORTY EIGHTH

Well lookee here, what do you know?
Aren't you the lucky so and so,
When birthdays fall on Mother's day,
It's poor old Dads who have to pay.

Washing dishes, scrubbing floors,
Doing all the household chores,
While Lady Muck with smug expression,
Deals out jobs in quick succession.

The trouble is, it's so frustrating,
And I've done some rapid calculating,
But never do I once remember,
A Father's day in mid—December.

So I guess I'll never get the chance,
To lead our Mum a merry dance,
To issue orders from a chair,
I really think it's most unfair.

So Dad will have to grin and bear it,
Pity the kids aren't here to share it,
So I'll wear my most disarming smile,
And try to make this day worthwhile.

So happy birthday dear one,
And very many more to come,
And after all, what's in a name,
I guess I'd spoil you just the same.

FORTY NINTH

Once more I take my pen to write,
And concentrate with all my might,
'Cos March the twenty fourth is near,
And it's poem time again I fear.

This day is yours above the rest,
A day of laughter, joy and jest,
So with your morning cup of tea,
Read these lines of verse from me.

May each hour bring a nice surprise,
A happy face and sparkling eyes,
With gifts and birthday cards and wine,
For my darling who is forty nine.

FIFTIETH

For all the days this coming year,
I wish you pathways strewn with flowers,
Freedom from all doubt and fear,
Tranquil and serene the hours,
Your birthday comes when spring awakes.

To banish signs of winter's gloom,
Over hills; in fields; by lakes,
Daffodils and crocus' bloom,
And though you've reached autumnal grace,
let still spring lingers in your face.

FIFTY FIRST

At last the longed for day is here,
Happy birthday Vicki dear,
We've both looked forward to this day,
But in a different sort of way.

For you the day means getting spoiled,
Staggering home at night well oiled,
Lemon pie, mixed fruit and jelly,
Opening the parcels under the telly.

But for me the day Will mean at last,
Those quips about my age have passed,
For on this day we reach the stage,
When, once more, we're the self—same age.

And so for nine more months they'll be,
Peace and perfect harmony,
Until, once more, that 'dig' I'll hear,
'But you are so much older dear.

So until that day, my wish to you,
Is happiness the whole year through,
May your sweetest, dearest dreams come true,
And may I share them all with you.

FIFTY SECOND
VICKI'S DAY

We celebrate the birth of Christ,
His rising at Easter too,
We spare a thought for those who fought,
And the courage of the few.

On St. George's day we wear a rose.
On St. David's day a leak,
The first of May is Labour day,
And a wake can last a week.

There's Mother's day and Father's day,
And famous victories,
And some, I hear, can last a year,
Like Silver Jubilees.

But the day that means the most to me,
Occurs in early spring,
When the sun grows warm, and the fresh leaves form,
And larks and linnets sing.

That day is March the twenty fourth,
So let the flags unfurl,
Let the people shout, and the bells ring out,
For a Happy Birthday girl.

FIFTY THIRD

May this birthday be a happy one ,
Packed with gaiety and fun,
No somber thoughts your mind assail,
Let happiness and joy prevail.

Let the sun shine from a sky of blue,
Wakening springtime flowers anew,
Their colour and fragrance to display,
And decorate your breakfast tray.

Dad and kids all think of you,
Wish you health with a drink or two,
While in the evening, off we go
For dinner out with Wal and Flo.

And so my wish for you is this,
A day of happiness and bliss,
A day to keep in memory's store,
And only one of many more.

In loving Memory

FIFTY FOURTH

I hope today will prove to be,
A happy and a joyful one,
A daytime spent in sweet content,
And the evening hours in fun.

Presents in the morning light,
Tonight we dine at eight,
food, good wine - what sheer delight,
To forget for once our weight.

So the toast today is 'YOU' my dear,
Health and happiness sublime,
My love too will accompany you,
From now until the end of time..

FIFTY FIFTH

Once again, come rain or shine ,
At birthday time I pen a rhyme,
For if the words she reads aren't mine,
I'll be heading for a right hard time.

So how shall I phrase this little verse?
Will it be long or will it be terse?
Shall I tell of bowers of flowers?
Or describe the gentle April showers.

Shall I compare thee a dew drenched rose?
Or some such Elizabethan prose,
But hold! I'm not a love - sick swain,
Pouring out his love in vain.

This is a birthday message, pure and simple,
Not an eulogy to a maiden's dimple,
So banish the puzzled frown and smile,
While I continue in the age - old style.

May this year bring happiness galore,
Of one thing you'll be pleased, I'm sure,
Now my ascendancy is past,
And our ages are the same at last.

FIFTY SIXTH

On this very special day,
May good things come and go your way,
May the hours be spent in sweet content,
And joy be yours in work and play.

May everything you wish come true,
Success in everything you do,
May all you require be your heart's desire,
And the sun shine from a sky of blue.

May ne'er a jarring word be spoke,
By thoughtless, inconsiderate folk,
May friends be true and remember you,
And regale you with a chat and joke.

So happy birthday dearest one,
And when your special day is done,
May you close your eyes with happy sighs,
And dream of all those hours of fun.

FIFTY SEVENTH (THE ELUSIVE DAY)

March contains a special day,
But what it is, I cannot say,
I know it's round about this time,
That I have to write a sort of rhyme.

Now, let me see, what can it be?
That triggers me instinctively,
To grab some paper and a pen,
And furiously give thought again.

Give thought I say - give thought to what?
What can it be that I've forgot?
How can I write when there's no plot?
And it's me, I think, who's to be shot.

'Cos I've got this nasty, sneaky feeling,
That a great sword dangles from the ceiling,
And if I don't find something soon to write,
It'll drop on me from a great big height.

Now, what event of celebration,
Can cause such gloomy consternation?
What occasion filled with joy,
Could be fraught with risk for Barrie boy?

And March contains a lot of days,
Which fill the bill in many ways,
But half of them have gone, and so,
We're left with just a few to go.

As each day passes, these get fewer,
It can't be Easter, I am sure,
So eliminating all the rest,
The twenty fourth sounds much the best.

My goodness yes, that strikes a chord,
I'm reminded strongly of - oh lord!
Don't tell me now, just let me guess,
It's dear old Vicki's birthday — yes?

so now I know I must pen,
A little birthday ode again,
so then, without much more ado,
Here's a little verse for you.

May all things be for your delight,
May all you do and say be right,
And may this day be one long mirthday.
On this your fifty seventh birthday.

FIFTY EIGHTH

Good birthday morn my little one,
May the day ahead be full of fun,
And blissfully every hour spent,
In happiness and sweet content.

But make the most of it my sweet,
For on this day our ages meet,
No longer can you say with truth,
'Compared to you, I am a youth.'

Today we both are fifty eight,
And now that preferential state,
Enjoyed so much since Christmas last,
Is now a relic of the past.

And the old stock phrase that once came pat,
'I'm younger than you, I can't do that,
Is no more valid, equality is here,
Your age has caught up with you, my dear.

But, never mind, you have this day,
Enjoy it darling while you may,
For I shall keep you well in line,
Until the day I'm fifty nine.

FIFTY NINTH

In this ever changing world,
Some things still remain,
Spring still brings the buds and flowers,
And your birthday comes again.

How lucky are those favored few,
Who waking on this special morn,
Find the Earth has woken too,
And a brand new season's born.

Unlike those of us who wake,
Upon our special day,
And wish the Lord above would take,
All that nasty snow away.

May all your days this coming year,
Be fresh and green as spring,
And I wish you all the joys, my dear,
That love and spring can bring.

SIXTY GLORIOUS YEARS

The year was nineteen twenty six,
A general strike had gripped the land,
Chaplin and Keaton were up to their tricks,
And your very first birthday was close at hand.

Hitler came to power in nineteen thirty three,
And so began a reign of fear,
The Nazi jackboot crushed the free,
And all this on your seventh year.

This year Britain had two kings,
Edward and George - it's thirty seven,
The big bands played and Crosby sings,
And our little girl is now eleven.

And now it's nineteen thirty nine,
The clouds of war have burst at last,
Vicki's well and doing fine,
She's thirteen now, and growing fast.

And now the people dance with joy,
Finished are the years of strife,
In forty four you met a boy,
One day you'll be his wife.

You married the boy in forty seven,
Both happy, proud and gay,
Lovers reaching for that piece of heaven,
That now seemed not so far away.

In Malta your first son was born,
And when the tour abroad was done,
To Croft alone and all forlorn,
The year was nineteen fifty one.

Then Chris was born in fifty two,
And Grahame in fifty three,
Everest climbed, the Queen crowned too,
And we all went off to Germany.

So past the fifties in content,
The swinging sixties came and went,
The seventies was a time of growth,
When Dave and Grahame pledged their troth.

So Vicki Cooke, this is your life,
And as another birthday nears,
I raise my glass to my dear wife,
And sixty glorious years.

In loving Memory

SIXTY FIRST

In winter's mantle snugly wrapped,
The shrubs and tree tops snowy capped,
In spring the young shoots struggle through,
Buds and blossoms burst anew.

In summer flowers bloom again,
Warmed by sun and cooled by rain,
In autumn nature's storehouse fills,
Light frost forms on vales and hills.

Mild days mingle with the cold,
Signs the year is growing old,
But soon the spring returns again,
The winter's snows melt into rain.

The pageantry of seasons going,
Like a river, ever onward flowing,
And so with each succeeding year,
Another birthday time draws near.

Each one a cause for celebration,
And an early morning recitation,
A ritual observed each year,
For me to wish you joy and cheer.

And so from dawn's first light, 'till day is done,
Have a happy birthday Mum.

SIXTY SECOND

It's someone's birthday,
Can't think who,
She's trim and dark,
And five feet two.

Her nose is cute,
Her eyes are blue,
And on this day,
She's sixty two.

So look around the room,
And if there's no one else in view,
The description that I give,
Can apply to only you.

So now I've found my birthday girl,
My wish this day for you,
Is happiness and sweet content,
And joy the whole day through.

SIXTY THIRD

We're off today for the Easter hols,
To spend some time at Flo and Wal's,
But, before we go I'd like to say,
Have a happy day today.

And on this happy birthday morn,
May the joy start with the breaking dawn,
And every waking moment spent,
In happiness and sweet content.

And one more thing I'd like to mention,
It is my hope and my intention,
To wish that at the same time you,
Will have a happy Easter too.

SIXTY FOURTH

Happy birthday 'little one,'
I hope today will bring much fun,
With lots of pleasant things to do,
And happiness the whole day through.

Forget the world and all its care,
This is the day we both can share,
Your slightest wish I'll make my cause,
Name it and the thing is yours.

We have each other, come what may,
And we'll make this one a lovely day,
And may the days that follow on,
Be as happy as the one just gone.

SIXTY FIFTH

Sixty five today. Retirement year is here,
So put your feet up; settle down,
And, like me, take it easy dear.

But in a home where both retire,
Who will do the household chores,
This means each morn we must enquire,
Is it my turn, dear, today or yours.

So welcome to this blissful state,
May it last a long, long time,
And may your life be, from this date,
As happy, dear, as mine.

SIXTY SIXTH

Once more it's birthday time my dear,
I'm sorry that it comes with pain,
The days seem dark and oh, so drear,
And I pray the sun soon shins again.

But forget your woes just for today,
Have a carefree time with friends,
Dine and drink and laugh and may,
The day bring joy and make amends.

SIXTY SEVENTH

Today we celebrate anew,
The anniversary of your birth,
Sixty seven years for you,
Upon God' s green and pleasant Earth.

Every year made more complete,
By the fact that you were there,
And many days made bitter sweet,
By a love we both would share.

So once more it's 'Happy birthday dear,
May all your dreams come true,
And for this and each successive year,
May I share them all with you.

SIXTY EIGHTH

Once again your birthday time has come,
Once again you've reached my age,
Three months I've been the senior one,
And now you've reached that self-same stage.

So, equal once again we go,
Through one more birthday year,
And there is one thing sure I know,
That I'll be always near.

So, have a happy birthday dear,
Let not trials and tribulations,
And all those little things you fear,
Mar your birthday celebrations.

SIXTY NINETH

Of all the days that span the phase,
Of the year that's come and gone,
There is no doubt, some days stand out,
As those when the sun truly shone.

In loving Memory

Then there are the days of blacks and greys,
When depression and misery abound,
When we think there's no end to this horrible blend,
Some light in the darkness is found.

Sunshine streams through that small patch of blue,
And lifts up our hearts once again,
And so it all goes, as the year ebbs and flows,
And sunshine follows the rain.

But, among all the rest, there's the one I like best,
And it doesn't depend on the weather,
It comes in the spring, when the birds start to sing,
And it's one we can both share together.

It's the day you were born, and right from that morn,
The world was a little bit brighter,
You lightened each place with your mischievous face,
And drew the strings of my heart ever tighter.

So bang the drums in celebration, voices raised in jubilation,
Extol her virtues far and near,
And while they sing, this wish I bring,
Your skies this day stay blue and clear.

SEVENTIETH

Come sleepy head, stretch and yawn,
Draw the curtains, face the morn,
Today's a special day you know,
And everything must be just so.

So here, my dear, to start the day,
Your breakfast laid out on a tray,
Pampered, petted, spoiled you'll be,
By all your friends and family.

And to complete this special day,
There's Crystal and Stewart here to stay,
At noon we'll wander in a bunch,
To the Castle and partake of lunch.

And there, with champagne glasses raised,
We'll toast this happiest of days,
And when, at last, the day is done,
We'll wish you many more to come.

SEVENTY FIRST

What can I say on this special day,
That hasn't been said before?
What songs can I sing? What gifts can I bring?
To add to your treasure store.

No songs, no gifts, but a love sincere,
A tenderness and a hope you'll find,
On this day and throughout the year,
Happiness and peace of mind.

SEVENTY SECOND

To be sung to the tune of 'Happy days are here. again'

Birthday time is here again,
A day of cheer and pink champagne,
And we'll drink and sing that old refrain,
Happy birthday Vicki dear.

A day of laughter, gifts and flowers,
And joy throughout your waking hours,
May the sunshine banish all the showers,
On your birthday Vicki dear.

SEVENTY THIRD

Now is the time for one more rhyme,
To celebrate this day so fine,
And trust that every hour may bring,
The sights and sounds and tastes of spring.

May this birthday be a happy one,
From early morn 'til day is done,
May all your dreams be realized,
Have everything you idolize.

May peace and tranquil hours prevail,
May aspirations never fail,
And perhaps, with luck, the sun will shine,
On this birthday dear old dutch of mine.

SEVENTY FOURTH

I take up pen to write again,
Another birthday rhyme ,
To wish you joy and free from pain,
In this millennium time.

Is there jam and cakes for tea?
Jellies and goodies abound,
Party hats for you and me,
Happy laughter all around.

But, those were the birthdays of our youth,
Now, I'm very much afraid,
And indeed, to tell you all the truth,
Today they are more staid.

And so for the sake of Auld Lang Syne (*1),
I'll raise my glass and drink a toast,
Here's to a happy birthday time,
For the one I love the most.

SEVENTY FIFTH

Our girl is seventy five today,
Beat the drum and shout hooray,
It's been a long haul to this day I guess,
From way back in nineteen twenty six no less.

Three quarters of a century has flown,
Seven and a half decades you've known,
Years of peace and war and love,
And deep content with what you have.

Retired but hasn't gone to ground,
She meets her friends and shops around,
She leads a healthy, active life,
She has her ills but copes with strife.

Now on the anniversary of her birth,
I wish her joy and lots of mirth,
She is my sweet and dear old dutch,
And tell her I love her very much.

SEVENTY SIXTH

I'm not a very good poet,
But it is your birthday time,
And so it falls to me,
To compose a birthday rhyme.

Over the years of joy and tears ,
I've written many a verse,
Sometimes my rhymes one hears,
Are bad and sometimes worse.

But they are written from the heart, my dear,
And that's the thing that counts,
So this verse I write to you this year,
Is sincere by all accounts.

So, happy birthday dearest one,
All smiles, no tears to weep,
And when, at last, the day is done,
Sweet dreams enfold your sleep.

SEVENTY SEVENTH

The time has come around at last,
To pen a rhyme as in the past,
To celebrate this happy day,
And keep the miseries away.

So a happy seventy seventh my dear,
May this be a lucky year,
May all your dearest dreams come true,
And health and happiness for you.

Farewell then my little one,
My poem for this month is done,
But, be sure too that come what may,
I'll pen some more another day.

SEVENTY EIGHTH

I've conversed with the muse, to help me to use,
My wit to write you a poem,
The words are there, swirling around in the air,
And the verses keep coming and going.

So I pluck some from here and I take some from there,
And I try to make sense of the jumble,
Then, lo and behold, they start to unfold,
And begin to make sense as they tumble.

They dress up in lines and begin to form lines,
And now we're getting somewhere,
So why all the flurry, 'cos I 'm in a hurry',
It's someone's birthday you see.

And I wish to extend, as I will to the end,
Birthday greetings as ever from me.

So, a happy seventy eighth my love,
May your day be made in heaven above,
And with many, many more to come,
Before my rhyming days are done.

SEVENTY NINTH

Once more I'm brought to mind,
It's Vicki's birthday time,
I've tried to search my mind to find,
A suitable birthday rhyme.

But the only words that's in my brain,
Are the ones sincere and true,
So I write just once again,
Happy birthday my love to you.

And so it goes until next time,
When I pen another birthday rhyme,
May the days that's in between be great,
May you enjoy each one with me, your mate.

In loving Memory

EIGHTYETH

There comes a time in every man's life,
When he has to arrange a party for his lovely wife,
Phone calls here and phone calls there,
People to be contacted everywhere.

All our friends and all our relations,
All to receive their special invitations,
This, I admit, I have to shirk,
'Cos Grahame's done all that work.

Now to arrange a blinking date,
We'll have to have it a day late,
'Cos someone's just popped up to say,
Mother's day's only two days away.

Now let's hope that upon the day,
That everything will be OK,
With a goodly crowd assembled there,
Friends and relations everywhere.

So what else remains for me to say,
But have a very happy day,
For this your 80th event,
Special day — heaven sent.

EIGHTY FIRST

'tis birthday time again,
My brow is creased in pain,
Trying to compose a poetic rhyme,
To go with this auspicious time.

My brow is cleared,
It's not as bad as I had feared,
All I do is to write a line,
Which says 'Happy Birthday' time.

EIGHTY SECOND

Happy Birthday Vicki dear ,
May the happiness last all year,
You've reached the age of eighty two,
Now you've got to my age too.

I'm no more boss around the house,
From now on I'm as quiet as a mouse,
You've never been eighty two before,
And I pray you'll have many more.

APPENDIX &
Additional Information

Citations

*1 Auld Lang Syne is a poem written by Robert Burns in 1788 and set to the tune of a traditional folk song (Roud# 6294). It is well known in many countries, especially in the English-speaking world, its traditional use being to bid farewell to the old year at the stroke of midnight on New Year's Eve.

Family History

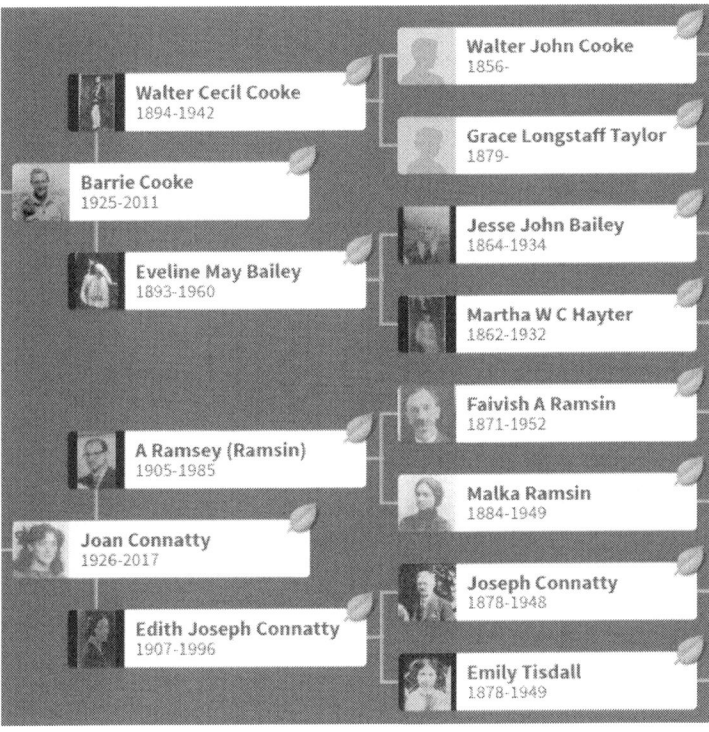

I have researched our family tree extensively, in order to fully understand someone, their personality, intelligence, traits or integrity its important to know where they come from. The following is a list of currently published books and works on the history of Barries family I've found.

1. The Letterbook of Richard Crawshay 1788-1797
2. Cyfarthfa and the Crawshays - 31 Dec 1999
3. The Crawshays of Cyfarthfa Castle: A Family History- 1967

The Crawshays coat of arms (above)

Printed in Poland
by Amazon Fulfillment
Poland Sp. z o.o., Wrocław